Swimming in Oblivion:

New and Selected Poems

Swimming in Oblivion:

New and Selected Poems

By
Howie Good

REDHAWK
PUBLICATIONS

SWIMMING IN OBLVIVION:
NEW AND SELECTED POEMS

Copyright © 2022 Howie Good

All rights reserved. This book or parts thereof may not be reproduced in any form, stored in any retrieval system, or transmitted in any form by any means—electronic, mechanical, photocopy, recording, or otherwise—without prior written permission of the publisher, except as provided by United States of America copyright law. For permission requests, write to the publisher, at "Attention: Permissions Coordinator," at the address below.

Redhawk Publications
The Catawba Valley Community College Press
2550 US Hwy 70 SE
Hickory NC 28602

ISBN: 978-1-952485-97-8

Library of Congress Number: 2022948039

Cover Design & Layout: Jamie Bruckmann
Cover Image: Patricia Thompson

redhawkpublications.com

Table of Contents

Howie Good's Path of Most Resistance:
An Appreciation by Mike James

New Poems	1
War Without Rules	2
Mood Piece	3
What Happens When You Don't Wear Green	4
Making Love	5
Memory Upgrade	6
Memento Mori	7
A Whole New Ball Game	8
Love Was Infinitely Shining	9
The Anxiety Index	10
The Day Before Yesterday	11
Ninety-Nine Times Out of a Hundred	12
Trick of the Eye	13
Evening Walk	14
The Visitation	15
Murderers on Holiday	16
Green Yellow Red	17
Origin Story	18
Where We Are	19
Ambrose Bierce Walks at Midnight	20
Daliesque	21
The Quality of Mercy Is Not Strained	22
Imaginary Landscape No. 1	23
Yes, Dr. No	24
After Magritte	25
Swimming in Oblivion	26
TV Land	27
Regime Change	28
Before the Fall	29
Drowning on Dry Land	30
Foreboding Music	31
Machiavellian	32
Ghost Guns	33

The Texture of Experience	34
Fog Area	35
Dry Spell	36
Meds	37
Ashes to Ashes	38
Rocks	39
Interview Questions for a Job Yet to Be Invented	40
'No Animals Were Harmed. . .'	41
Life Story	42
Unfunny Valentine	43
Birds of New England, Revised Edition	45
Country Noir	46
All Good Stories End in Death, Hemingway Said	47
A Chronic Condition	48
Change in the Weather	49
Stairs to Nowhere	50
Death Be Not Proud	51
Re: Vision	52
Stolen Horses	53
A Blow to the Heart	54
Street of Crocodiles	55
Death Trains	56
Family Tree	57
Making Lunch	58
All About Me	59
E = MC Escher	60
Dead Relatives	61

Selected Poems — 62

Red Rosa	63
The Rigorous Sadness of Erik Satie	64
Oscar Wilde's Teeth	65
Art for Art's Sake	66
French Cool	67
Advice for the Perplexed	68
The End of Nature	69
The Third Reich of Dreams	70

Heartsick	71
Well, Well, Well	72
Myths of the Near Future	73
Claw	74
The View from Here	75
Fire Burns Upwards	76
Safety Instructions for the Twenty-First Century	77
A New Kind of Heaven	78
A Hazy Shade of Postcolonial Melancholia	79
Kiss Your Ass Goodbye	80
Grandson	81
The Importance of Listening	82
Wheatfield with Crows	83
Oh, Mercy	84
The Ladder	85
Love Note	86
The Carnival of Being	87
Pastiche	88
Hotel of Forgotten Artists	89
Devolving	91
Certain Machines	92
The Flaw	93
Orogeny	95
The Heart of It All	96
In Excelsis Gloria	97
Lovesick	98
Acknowledgments	99
About the Author	100

Howie Good's Path of Most Resistance: An Appreciation

It's not dark yet, but it's getting there.
-Bob Dylan

During his brilliant and destructive youth, Steve Earle (singer-songwriter extraordinaire) once proclaimed, "Townes Van Zandt is the best songwriter in the whole world, and I'll stand on Bob Dylan's coffee table in my cowboy boots and say that." Later, older and sober. Earle recanted such unorthodoxy and admitted that Van Zandt was not as good as the forever mutable Dylan.

What does this story, which sounds almost apocryphal, have to do with the prose poetry of Howie Good? Well, like Steve Earle talking about Van Zandt, Good's prose poems summon similar hyperbolic and unorthodox statements. In his varied landscapes which encompass the political, the personal, the pop, the historical, and the surreal, Good's prose poems are unique in American literature.

Unlike the masterful prose poems of Robert Bly and James Wright, his work is seldom vatic. The characters which occupy his poems believe in horror more than transcendence. The god he comes across is "absorbed in his own thoughts" and acts "like he didn't believe he ought to exist." Within these poems, as in life, the mundane and the awful happen side-by-side. People die or climb a tree to survive, but hope left on a train to an unnamed camp long ago.

The world Good creates is both visual (he loves to reference painters) and apocalyptic. His work does not re-state the commonplace. A reader will not think, "I have also felt this way." Instead, Good offers a kaleidoscope view of another reality which often bleeds into our own.

None of this is to imply that his work is without humor. Good often laughs at himself, but his humor is not like vaudeville. It is like the existential jokes of Steven Wright or the ironic jokes of Franz Kafka or the exit door jokes of the patient in the cancer ward. Even his many book titles like *The Bad News First, The Titanic Sails at Dawn,* and *The Death Row Shuffle* display his dark humor. Sometimes Good's characters laugh until they cry and then they keep crying.

It's important to say characters since these poems are occupied by various figures. There's no self-willed persona in Good's work as there is in the work of Bukowski and his acolytes. Only the constancy of themes (fear of the unknown, the certainty of pain and death, the cruelty of existence, and the occasional redemption of art) reveal anything about the man behind the writing.

In his essay, "A Small Note on Prose Poetry," Good wrote, "All poetry worthy of the name exists in opposition to the churn of mass culture." The idea of opposition is the force behind Good's work and aesthetic. He writes as an outsider who makes arguments against the easy and expected.

Good's background in journalism gives a clarity to his work even when he seems to take notes from a made-up country. Journalism taught him the value of a strong declarative sentence and he is a solid student of the ways a sentence can be shaped.

Good's outsider status is confirmed in his life and in his poetry. He's a bit like Alfred Starr Hamilton: tied to no group or school, he has few readers and fewer supporters, but many fine poems. His writing career includes approximately 40 books from small and tiny presses in the United States and England, but involves neither an MFA program nor a WPA conference. Since no one told Good what kind of poems he should write, he went off and wrote like no one else.

Uniqueness is both difficult and rare. Howie Good's work is not difficult, but it is rare in the quality of the language, the vibrancy of the images, and the challenges of the worldview. What he offers the reader is a tilt-a-whirl ride where the landscape is always changing and where frogs rain in abundance.

Mike James

New Poems

War Without Rules

There were days when the explosions didn't subside. The sirens became more and more frequent, especially at night. We began to sleep badly. Then one morning, while hurrying to the market, I was struck by flying debris. At the hospital the doctor first looked around to make sure no one was listening who shouldn't be. "I just need to grab a lab coat and one egg and I can fix this," he said. He cut my feet open and put pennies in the incisions before sewing them back up and wrapping them in bandages. He said they were lucky pennies.

Mood Piece

Nights seemed darker back then. I resigned myself to long empty hours of insomnia. Someone said, "Have you been checked out by a psychiatrist recently?" The house across the street from ours was strung with Christmas lights way into spring. Police treated any outdoor gathering of three or more people as a riot. The latest idea in art was that only after a painter destroyed a painting, scratched it out, was it ready to be seen. A life's work could just about fit inside a shoebox.

What Happens When You Don't Wear Green

Other people are just shadows. Many haven't heard about Syria. They say, "Where is Syria?" Some think it's Siberia. You feel numb. Even when someone is telling you a joke you know is funny, you can't laugh. Every day there's a funeral — sometimes several at once. And the dead are all so young. The bodies come to you in bad condition, covered in dirt, blood, open wounds. Shots to the knees tell you the person was tortured. Sometimes it's really hard to put the parts of the body together. You try, but it's not something three drunk dudes can do with a hammer.

Making Love

Sometimes it's like the slow, patient unraveling of the obscure meaning of a passage in a sacred text, and other times more like kids in their parents' cars doing donuts in an empty parking lot, simple noisy fun, and afterwards, when everything has finally stopped spinning, we experience a floating feeling, as if our bodies have become indistinguishable from the golden haze that surrounds them.

Memory Upgrade

My mother flushed my goldfish down the toilet while I was at school. I had won the fish at a carnival by tossing a ping-pong ball into the fish's bowl. Memory needs to tell some kind of story. The story might not be evident, but it has to be there. Buddy Holly at his show in Duluth three days before the plane crash that killed him looked right at my mother when my mother was pregnant with me.

Memento Mori

I have to force myself to continue looking down at the dead fish that the tide has washed ashore. The gulls have been at it and the crabs and now the fat black flies. In fact, it's so mutilated I can't tell what kind of fish it was – a fluke? a porgy? – its skin rotting off and its delicate bones obscenely exposed. A little way up the beach, sunbathers sprawl on towels, children dig in the sand, the lifeguard on the lifeguard tower blows a whistle. The land has no memory of having once been ocean.

A Whole New Ball Game

The catcher tears off his hockey-style mask to go after a foul pop-up and the skin of his face gets torn off with it. Meanwhile, a dirigible emblazoned with a death's skull logo comes slowly floating over the stadium. The umpire behind the plate points up and signals for timeout and then flees the field, setting off a general rush toward the exits. Women are knocked down and children trampled, but vendors in the stands just go on howling, *Beer here! Beer here!* It's like someone has dropped in unexpectedly, told you their dreams, and wants you, the average fan, to interpret them.

Love Was Infinitely Shining

My wife and I were sitting with our coffee at a little square table in the window of the bakery/café. We could hear gunfire in the distance, militiamen shooting into alleys and cellars where illegals might be hiding. "The soul of man prevails," my wife quoted as we sat there, "but only when moral struggle is present." Any wonder I love her? I blew on my coffee and carefully took a sip. The hour's top headlines were crawling across the bottom of the big screen TV on the wall: *Disgraced NY Congressman Resigns, Japan's Sakurajima Volcano Erupts, Pope Prays for Peace.* Bursts of gunfire repeated in a periodic pattern, similar to a beating heart.

The Anxiety Index

Then one night I dreamt I was dead and looking for my grave. I looked in the gray, frozen streets Kafka used to walk. My bones crunched with each step. My eyes rattled in their sockets. I wanted to cry out, "I don't belong here, I don't!" but couldn't because my childhood stutter had returned even worse than I remembered. The clock on the city hall tower moved neither backwards nor forwards. I encountered Kafka outside on the steps. "Where's the moon in the Moonlight Sonata?" I shouted in his face. Deep red drops of blood dripped on a bunch of white daisies.

The Day Before Yesterday

Meanwhile, Franz Kafka sells another piece of his dead mother's jewelry to pay for his brothel visits. Pablo Picasso and Henri Matisse go horseback riding together. Alma Mahler has just aborted their child. The police question Dr. Freud, but he has an alibi and they release him after slapping him around. Using an alias, Adolf Hitler boards a train for Munich to escape conscription in the Austro-Hungarian army. Summer is fading, and Rainer Maria Rilke feels it as a wound in his chest. Da Vinci's Mona Lisa has been missing now for months. Museumgoers lay flowers in front of the bare wall.

Ninety-Nine Times Out of a Hundred

Have you ever been in the shower when there was an earthquake? Dated a relative by accident? Wanted to eat toothpaste? Ripped off your pants while dancing? Been unable to recognize your own reflection in the mirror or differentiate between faces and objects? It's like walking into a hallucination without being quite sure whose it is. I kind of wish Baudelaire were alive to see it. Under the turmoil of a violet gray sky, there's a fire made of people.

&

When I complain of crippling back pain, the doctor just says that's what it's like to be a person in this world. Regardless, I get a postcard in the mail guaranteeing me a chance to win one of 1,000 prizes. Me! The man who was once stung by a dead bee! Meanwhile, the children exchange conspiratorial glances across the dinner table, their eyes like burn holes.

&

They're auctioning off the unwashed and still stained underwear Elvis wore on stage beneath his iconic white jumpsuit. The darkness at the root of things inevitably seeps to the surface. I try ignoring my yearning for something better or at least different, but I can't, any more than I could a rooftop sniper firing randomly into a crowd I had joined. And it's not like I'm a guy committed to the dictionary definition of words. What they call "hope" I would call a complete absence of twilight.

Trick of the Eye

Yesterday, as I was getting into my car, I saw in the sky the squarish letters of the Hebrew alphabet fringed in fire. Now I sat in an exam chair in a small windowless room filled with the loud hum of medical machines whose purpose would remain a mystery to me. Because of the noise, the eye doctor and his assistant used hand gestures to communicate with each other. They mimed tossing bombs, cutting throats, shoveling in food, counting out money. I knew right then that there was nothing actually wrong with my sight. It was just that I hadn't ever seen with such bleak clarity before.

Evening Walk

I'm walking the dog along a narrow strip of dirt, a kind of no man's land, between bare woods and the roadway. Although the clocks were set forward an hour a week ago, darkness is rapidly falling, as if every little town has its share of evil. When the dog squats, I take the couple of moments to look around. I like to see things that maybe I'm not supposed to see. But there are no strange truths or cryptic warnings detectable, only the faintest bulge of new buds on dead-seeming branches, the gnarled, knobby fingers of fierce invalids.

The Visitation

I heard a massive thump. Alarmed, I went to the sliding glass door and looked out, expecting to see a seagull lying there dead after crashing into the glass. Instead, a juvenile sand shark was flailing on the back deck. I couldn't have been more astonished if I'd been visited by an angel clothed in light or a neighbor wearing no clothes at all. The shark was just a foot long and battleship gray. As it thrashed about, I called to my wife, "Barbara, quick, bring a bucket!" I half-filled the bucket from the hose. Then Barbara, using a gardening trowel, managed to drop the shark into the bucket. This is the world. Whatever the hour, there's always a rendezvous going on.

Murderers on Holiday

I was born with holes in me. I can't visualize the love of our fellow man that the Bible preaches with the clarity I can baseball on the radio. If there were actually angels, would they fly in a V-formation like geese, you think? Crows can hold a grudge for a year or more against someone who has mistreated them. No one should feel particularly safe. I love cats, but even a cat, when it's starving, could eat a person.

Green Yellow Red

We live in the future, an ambitious developer's aborted dream. Abandoned shopping malls are being demolished or converted into holding pens and mental health clinics. Streets have been renamed for the streetwalkers murdered by Jack the Ripper: Mary Ann Nichols, Annie Chapman, Elizabeth Stride, etc. Most of the time the police are just amusing themselves. I slip in the door with a sense of relief, as if I've shaken off someone who's been tailing me. Later when I peek between the curtains, I discover children pecking in the grass like backyard chickens. If I knew how things would turn out, I would've run more yellow lights.

Origin Story

Puffed up with pride of authorship, I showed the newspaper clipping, with my name and age, 13, at the bottom in festive italics, to Mr. Eakely, my English teacher. He didn't even pretend to read it. "What's that?" he just said, pointing at the 13. "Your IQ?" The rest of the morning was strangely garbled. Car. Boat. Fire. Adrift.

Where We Are

Elephants in India are drinking wine and passing out in tea gardens. It's all anyone can talk about even as a flaming sword passes overhead. Birds fall out of the sky. Leaves on trees quickly wither. Roofs catch fire. In the days that follow, the sulfur smell of smoke doesn't dissipate but seeps into people's clothes and skin. No one thought any of this would ever happen. My wife and I look across the table at each other with only a tentative sense of recognition.

Ambrose Bierce Walks at Midnight

I recognized him from his picture in an old literature textbook. It had been over 100 years since he had mysteriously disappeared across the border. I asked where he had gone and why and what he had done there. He wouldn't answer. When I added I was a big fan of his writing, especially the Civil War tales, he just snickered. I didn't know what to say next but felt I had to say something. "You like being a ghost?" I asked. He gave me a sly little grin. "You get to sleep all day," he said, "so you can work at night."

Daliesque

It's bad luck, they say, to wake up a student who's fallen asleep in class, but if I don't, she may never know that the thesaurus lists some 140 synonyms for darkness or that the renegade Spanish artist Salvador Dali sat up on his deathbed and cursed the priest who had come to shrive him. I myself have thought of growing a moustache that curves fiercely down at the ends in homage to legendary brigands. "No gods, no masters / The revolution will be kingless," a graffitist has sprayed on a retaining wall where anyone passing can see it. So wake up, child, speak. The tongue is all muscle.

The Quality of Mercy Is Not Strained

Some 2,000 years ago, Julius Caesar ordered a gang of pirates he'd captured on the Mediterranean to be crucified, a form of punishment designed to produce a slow death with maximum humiliation and suffering. But just before the large wooden crosses to which the pirates had been tied were raised off the ground, Caesar, in an act of mercy, drew his knife and personally cut their throats.

&

In the camps, specially designated Jewish prisoners, the sonderkommandos, had to disentangle the naked corpses lying in heaps in the gas chambers and cart them to the ovens for cremation. Although the hair caught fire first, it was the head that took longest to burn.

&

A doctor compares the heart to a house with four doors. Others don't want to believe their own memories. The sky is gray, the ocean black. Bombs fall on a breadline, a theater, a maternity ward. Oh mankind, why do you destroy yourself? Up, you corpses! Get up!

&

I was born in the rain and the dark. The two atom bombs were dropped that summer. There was a poisonous glitter in the sky, and it went all over the world. Familiar words were given new, unfamiliar meanings. Wounds refused to heal. Roses might have been the size of bonfires.

&

We may think we know where we're going when we head out for the day, but we don't. A panhandler on the traffic island holds up a ragged piece of cardboard, *Beep if you know Jesus* shakily written on it in marker. Nobody does.

Imaginary Landscape No. 1

We used to do it on the floor, and up against a wall, and with you sitting on a stool. I miss our old spontaneous frenzies, trees rocking in the wind. Oh, sure, the past exists, but only as a ghostly tapping or as something to be looked at with one eye from the other side of the glass — an entire city of burning churches, soot and ash everywhere, and operators standing by 24/7.

Yes, Dr. No

After a preliminary exam, the eye doctor tells me to go sit in the waiting area while "the laser heats up," and for an instant, I'm not at the clinic on West Main or an anxious 70-year-old who has suddenly lost most of the vision in his left eye. I'm back in 1962. Sean Connery, as James Bond in *Dr. No,* is tied spreadeagle on a steel table, a laser weapon like a sci-fi Sword of Damocles poised above him. But even as the fiery red laser beam that cuts through metal creeps closer and closer and closer to his balls, he banters with the archvillain. Shortly it'll be my turn, and with the laser scorching the back of my eye, I'll whimper and writhe in the exam chair and discover the doubtful utility of his example of behaving courageously under make-believe circumstances.

After Magritte

A golden-haired woman is stretched out naked on the couch. Her throat has been cut. Blood from the gaping wound has leaked through the couch cushions and formed a puddle on the floor. A man in his mid- to late thirties, respectably dressed in a black suit, stands at a Victrola credenza, his back to the corpse. His blandly handsome face is expressionless as he watches as if mesmerized a recording by Caruso spin on the turntable. Unbeknownst to him, detectives, armed with nets and clubs, have taken up positions outside his door. The tension is palpable. Their faces are identical to his.

Swimming in Oblivion

The composer was sticking all sorts of things – bottle caps, tenpenny nails, forks and spoons, tortoise shell combs – in the strings of the Steinway in preparation for the night's performance. He followed the oft-abused philosophy that if you can't make art that is popular, you can at least make art that is perplexing. Later when he performed the piece, it would sound to some like a hellish chorus of rackety machines and to others like the crackle of gunfire.

&

It was getting shot through the neck while fighting against the fascists in Spain that completed George Orwell's political education. In the after years, the frontline trenches would be filled in and paved over or replanted with trees. The dead in their hundreds of thousands would possess only antiquarian interest for the living, if even that. Sea levels would rise, and labia cleavage become the hot new swimsuit trend.

&

The bomb bay doors are open, the bombs whistling down, the human targets below powerless to flee. We forget the most basic thing as if it were too complicated to remember: no person is safe where any person isn't.

TV Land

The veteran homicide detective with the Basset Hound face stands in a vacant lot, staring glumly down at a mutilated corpse dumped there overnight. Violent crime is common in this rust-pocked city, and the law itself often criminal. The detective sighs wearily. He searches his pockets for a cigarette before remembering he's quit smoking. A small plane flies over, pulling a large banner. He follows it with his eyes. SMILE EMPTY SOUL, the banner says. I'm no criminologist or any other kind of -ologist, but that's why I need to consult someone like him, who wants to watch the world burn, then save the people he loves.

Regime Change

Mother woke me up unusually early with the news that a lake of ash had appeared during the night and behind it a pair of wrinkled mountains like a giant's cracked, dusty boots. "Ah," I thought, "the cows. . . ." I couldn't have been more wrong. By the next day, men in trench coats and fedoras would be grabbing people right off the street and taking them away in unmarked cars. But, for now, there were steel bars on windows and suicide nets on roofs and a sign out front of the palace saying, Help Wanted / Apply Within.

Before the Fall

I was three years old, maybe four, lying on my stomach on the itchy wool carpet and filling with ecstatic scribbles the blank pages of an old business ledger my father had brought home from work, my future still void and formless, and my heart still a soft red peach without a savage bite taken out of it.

Drowning on Dry Land

I'm passing through the woods on foot. The map I follow exists only in my head. Three crows are keeping watch in a high oak tree. An uneasy feeling rustles the leaves. I stop to wait for the feeling to pass. The crows cackle at my obvious discomfiture. Later I'll realize I've never had reason to use the word "carapace" – the hard upper shell of a turtle, crustacean, etc. – in a sentence until now.

Foreboding Music

"On a scale of 1 to 10, with 1 being the lowest, how severe is your pain now?" the bouncy young medical assistant asks with misplaced enthusiasm. Fifty-eight friends on Facebook offer their thoughts and prayers. But just because my condition finally has a name doesn't mean it has a proven treatment. Cue foreboding music. An angel dressed in a clean white T-shirt and dirty jeans hums while grinding bones to make bread. The Lord remains out of sight in the palace. I sit down to replay a chess game and discover the pieces have been glued to the board.

Machiavellian

"Tell my father," Jesus's son said, "that if my devils leave me, my angels will take flight, too." And someone might've had it not been for the border patrols. There were just so many refugees trying to cross in the dark, and more coming all the time. The women had only ancient versions of the iPhone and dwindling food and water; the men, the shaved heads of conscripts or lobotomy patients. Children traveling on their own kept falling farther and farther behind, as though a vast apparatus was specifically arrayed against them. Machiavelli didn't say, "Lick the tire of my bicycle," but that's what he meant.

Ghost Guns

It was wartime. Cows in green gas masks stared at the sign outside one of the few churches still standing. Love Like Jesus, the sign said in changeable plastic letters. I scooped up a handful of parking lot gravel, intending to drive the cows off. The cows just stared at the sign and snickered and smelled like fresh-turned earth.

Two soldiers pushed along the road a parlor piano they had salvaged from the rubble. At the side of the road, an old woman was poking at a severed hand with her cane. It was spring. Birds whistled in the sun-dappled trees. The war made their happiness seem wrong.

Grandmothers, prodded by oaths and bayonets, were herded off the train and into wire pens. One confused old woman looked through the fencing at a heavily armed guard. "I know why you're here," she said, "but why am I?"

The Texture of Experience

The heat has been rising all day to an incinerating pitch. At the designated hour, I arrive at the address on foot, exhausted and dusty. It's an old, dingy residential hotel on a sunbaked street prowled by stray dogs, their every rib sharply outlined. When I look up, squinting against the glary sky, what appears to be an angel with a sword in its outstretched arm is hovering above the roof. *Nothing like this happens here,* a stranger who has materialized beside me says. I start to reply but can't. There are things that have no name even in the most poetic language.

Fog Area

I like to walk while I think. I'm thinking about the echoes of Socrates in Plato's Cave. A yellow road sign says Fog Area, but there is no fog. Trees have begun to put out leaves. Half-hidden among the leaves is a redwing blackbird, a small, dark shape with audacious jewellike markings. The bird keeps silent and still. It's the stillness of a Zen monk in meditation, it's the silence of a word from a lost language that has no English equivalent.

Dry Spell

Irreplaceable words are missing, have taken off for the Greek isles or maybe a peak in Darien or been kidnapped by an ad hoc gang of undistinguished small press poets, and with nothing now availing but the last syllables of an echo, I'm running falling flying floating crawling, and all the while all these birds calling out impossible directions.

Meds

Four gray gulls paddle about like ducks, the sky above the bay rapidly changing moods, darkening, then brightening, then darkening again, while I make my own path up the shoreline, careful despite a brain half-paralyzed from new meds to step around the conchs and horseshoe crabs stranded at low tide, too many for saving, a massacre, the water rushing away over the pebbly sand whispering to me, as though in consolation, shush, shush, shush.

Ashes to Ashes

A human body produces five pounds of ash when burned. Twenty-five tons of ash from the Topf & Sons ovens in the crematorium had been spread as fertilizer on the surrounding fields. Whenever the wind came whipping in, it would churn up a bitter brown smog of topsoil and ash that stung the skin and burned the nose and mouth and choked the lungs. Visibility shrank to almost nothing. Cart horses refused to budge and received terrible beatings from their enraged masters. Looters smashed shop windows. Countless frantic calls for help went unanswered. We look back and shake our heads and tell ourselves we aren't like those people. No, not at all.

Rocks

None of us even knew God had been dying this whole time until we got the news He was dead. A flash mob forced an old Jew to climb a tree and chirp like a bird. I was inside, tinkering with a machine I'd built for testing the concept that rocks communicate with each other. Despite a series of less than successful field trials, I wasn't ready to say yet whether it was the machine or the concept that was flawed. I removed the outer casing, replaced the circuit board. A choir on the classical music station was singing something John Milton wrote when he was going blind.

Interview Questions for a Job Yet to Be Invented

Have you ever demanded, received, or paid a ransom? Seen them kicking Edgar Allan Poe? Spent a night in the gorilla cage? Bought a human skull on Etsy? Shared an elevator with the eighteen smallest dwarfs in the city? Laughed so hard you dislocated your jaw? Asked Alexa the actual color of the Red Sea? (Intense turquoise.) Been bound and gagged and stuffed in a wheelie bin? Visited a parent in prison? Shrieked like a peacock or impersonated a disreputable poet with a pointy beard and long wool scarf? Dreamt you were dreaming? Put a smiley face at the end of a sentence? Hummed while performing cunnilingus?

'No Animals Were Harmed...'

Everywhere, chemicals. My house might as well be made of words for all the protection it affords. The previous tenant not only drank from the toilet, but also scrawled on the walls a disclaimer: "No animals were harmed in the making of this film." I wasn't laughing when my MRI came back showing frizzy orange hair and a painted frown. Since then, I have been insulating with crumpled newspaper. In this wind, faces have been eroded, lives uprooted and swept away. Apparently only grandmas with heavy bosoms have adequate ballast to keep to their feet.

Life Story

At birth I was given a name I wouldn't ever have chosen. The trick, I later discovered, is not to care. I was still in school when my parents died within a year of each other to make more room for the future. And I remember people throwing their hats in the air in jubilation. Until then, I too just wanted to bury everything that came before. Now I pass through crowds like a rumor. There's only one story but a million ways to tell it.

Unfunny Valentine

My heart is apocalyptically yours, a flag burned in protest, a kingdom composed of tiny but belligerent principalities, a SOS sent from deep space. It's a story told in jump cuts and flashbacks, the flashbacks arranged in alphabetic order. It's the 15 billion trees a year felled to make toilet paper. It's an amateurish forgery of that famous painting of young lovers floating through the sky locked in an embrace. It's a scar shaped somewhat like a tulip that's about to bloom.

Watching the News

I felt like a corpse pulled from a canal after three days in the water. Not our problem, the Supreme Court ruled, and ordered strangers deported and old-growth trees chopped down and the stumps dynamited. I might've adopted the code of the cowboy – *There's some things a man just can't ride around* – if only I'd been able to remember it at the time. A newborn had been abandoned in a toilet stall and another near a church, and both in the mistaken expectation they'd be found alive. That taught me as nothing else could to not watch the news so much. But my question to you is, If I've seen Georgia O'Keeffe naked in a gauzy black-and-white photograph by Stieglitz, have I really seen Georgia O'Keeffe naked?

Birds of New England, Revised Edition

I bought a book off the bargain table at Costco called *Birds of New England*. It's got detailed drawings of different kinds of birds – wading birds, songbirds, migratory birds. I still haven't been able to identify, though, the scruffy little bird the blue jays are always chasing away from our feeder. He's pathetic, like the panhandling wino who limped over to my car at a stoplight on Mass Ave. I didn't roll down the window. I didn't even look at him. I just sat there, waiting and waiting and waiting for the light to change.

Country Noir

A B-girl with sleepy, mud-colored eyes slipped onto the stool next to mine. "I am here to entertain you," she said and then added as a tease, "but only during my shift." At least she wasn't the kind of woman who would refer to poetry as "verse." I conspicuously returned my attention to the ball game on the widescreen TV over the bar. She leaned in closer and started to say something. I cut her off. It's not that I wasn't tempted; it's just that I'm cautious. Prison workshops and small rural cemeteries are filled with men who should have been.

All Good Stories End in Death, Hemingway Said

I didn't even know you were sick until I saw what your oldest posted on your Facebook page – that you had fallen into a coma during cancer treatment and were very near death. For a long moment, I wrestled with whether I should "Like" the post as an expression of support. It was the sort of dilemma that once would have had you shaking your head at me in mock despair. And now? The symphony that took all those years to compose has proved to take only about 17 minutes to perform.

A Chronic Condition

On this particular Sunday, a screaming crow flew across my path. The pope declared from his window in St. Peter's Square, "Don't be afraid of tattoos." Who was he trying to kid? When I walk, wherever I walk, my shadow walks ahead of me.

Change in the Weather

"Better call someone," I say to my wife, who is standing beside me at the window, peering up at the sky with a worried expression. By the time the emergency vehicles start arriving, the clouds look even more like insipid thoughts. All the commotion has drawn half the neighborhood out into the street. An upstairs neighbor I barely know tells me in a dunce-like voice that he has a titanium plate in his head. I give him a nervous smile. Death, when it finally comes, will have his phlegmy eyes.

Stairs to Nowhere

I was late for a class I taught at the college. When I dashed into the building where the class was held, the lobby was empty. I started up the main stairway. The stairs grew noticeably steeper the higher I climbed. By the time I reached the top, I was dry-mouthed and sweaty and convinced that something was badly wrong with my breathing. I had arrived on the outskirts of a country one only hears about when there is a coup or an earthquake or when a virus crosses the species barrier from animals to humans. Toothless old women in babushkas crowded around me. "If you must scream," one said, "scream quietly."

Death Be Not Proud

Drawn from accounts of near death experiences posted at Buzzfeed 1/4/2021

They told me I was dead for three minutes. I got hit by a car. There was a nice, dark nothingness, which felt kind of cozy, but I also knew it was the end, so I'd better not. Like, I wasn't supposed to be enjoying it, because if I embraced it too much, I would die. I looked up, and there was a bright light with a hand poking out making the "come here" gesture. I walked toward it and started hearing loud clanging and woke in the hospital. They told me I almost died. I said, "Oh yeah?" They explained a bunch of stuff and then offered me a grilled cheese. I had Doritos, too.

Re: Vision

"I'll lick stamps," I told the gargoyle from HR during the job interview. "I'll lick whatever you want." He shook his big, ugly head no. And as quick as that, I found myself back on the street. It had just started to rain when Jesus appeared. My first thought was that he looked nothing like his picture.

&

Horror is everywhere. If you go searching for some way to escape, you'll just end up in a 24-hour McDonald's beside a woman with fangs and a mustache. I'm not there even when I am, head crooked to the right, as if listening to the Carter Family sing "Wildwood Flower" via my metal fillings.

&

You who believe the most astounding lies, who wipe your behind and then sniff your fingers, the moon could look to you some nights like a shiny gold button dangling on a loose thread, but it never does.

Stolen Horses

My mother's mother's father was a milkman, like Tevye in *Fiddler on the Roof*. He had a sturdy pair of horses to pull his delivery wagon. One horse was white, my grandmother was telling me at her kitchen table, and the other was red. The Cossacks made off with the horses when they rampaged through the shtel on a pogrom. "They killed plenty Jews," my grandfather interjected in his mangled English, but my grandmother didn't seem to hear him. The horses, she said, were beautiful.

A Blow to the Heart

I dreamed the other night that dreaming had been outlawed. In my dream, an officer woke me with a blow to the heart. I saw to my horror that a traveling guillotine had already been assembled. Then, with the officer providing a running commentary, a technician made a hole in the top of my skull using an off-the-shelf cordless power drill. Something cold and cloudy floated up from the hole. "Only a memory," the officer said, sounding disappointed. When the police left, they took the memory with them in a cage.

Street of Crocodiles

The pills I take at night to get to sleep leave me feeling dazed all morning. I stare stupidly at the blank screen of my laptop while rubbing my head in a forlorn attempt to stimulate the language center of the brain. I think again of Bruno Schulz. Only the first sentence of the novel he was writing when he was murdered survives: *Mother awakened me in the morning, saying, "Joseph, the Messiah is near. . . ."* A Gestapo officer shot him down in the street in broad daylight. It was a kind of hobby, to be honest.

Death Trains

Chimpanzees living in captivity have been known to defiantly throw their turds at their keepers, and so it was that as he looked out on the rail yard where special police in black uniforms enforced the loading of a long line of boxcars, the fussy little clerk with a clipboard was very glad that people aren't like chimps.

Family Tree

I was born in the rain and dark. "Cure me or kill me," I begged the doctors in attendance. But apparently only when silent was I able to be heard. I'd been assembled by someone who couldn't be bothered to read the assembly instructions. Seventy years later, I look in the mirror and see bits and pieces of a stranger's face – a long, fleshy nose, protuberant eyes, a domelike Shakespearean forehead. My now grown children stand well off to the side, uncertain whether to huddle or flee. As I tentatively approach, I clutch a rose, shoulder high like a dagger.

Making Lunch

Jack Kerouac came up with the title *Naked Lunch* for William S. Burroughs' now-famous novel. Allen Ginsberg, who was editing the book with Kerouac, asked what the title meant. Kerouac said they would figure that out later. And Burroughs? He was in the kitchen cutting the crust off reality sandwiches.

All About Me

A mumbling wino in a ratty overcoat stops me on the sidewalk outside Kappy's Liquor. It's a sunny afternoon, but he brings with him his own weather, gray and dank. I try not to appear angry or alarmed by his presence. He asks for bus fare, says he's stranded, his car's got a flat. This is obviously a lie. On the other hand, we are all on the road, all kicking up the same dust. He looks at me with begging eyes. I don't need to speak. I just shake my head no.

E = MC Escher

Einstein's colleagues at the Institute of Advanced Study were worried that he was drinking again. Without a word of warning to anyone, he had shaved off his spectacular mane of wild white hair. Now he was openly talking about getting a tattoo of e=mc2 on his neck. In addition, he had started bringing his pet raven, Poe, to the office. No one knew then that while some guest lecturer stood at the board bloviating, he would sit there in the audience listening with foreboding to something only he could hear – the steady ticking of the universe's cooling engine.

Dead Relatives

One rejected the whole concept of sin but admitted the existence of evil. Another would have preferred Braille to e-books. A third had a fluty voice only while on the phone. A fourth referred to our annual family reunion as "Kafkaesque." A fifth and sixth didn't know which truth was the right truth to follow. A seventh put black tar heroin on his to-do list. An eighth would knock just once and then leave if the door wasn't opened immediately. My dead. There have been years when I haven't been able to visit you. There are days like this when that's all I do.

Selected Poems

Red Rosa

For Rosa Luxemburg

She lost a shoe as they dragged her from the Hotel Eden to a waiting car. Lieutenant Vogel, commander of the unit, shouted insults ("Whore!") and spat at her. She was bleeding from a blow to the head with a rifle butt, but could still see with the eye that didn't have blood in it. As they were putting her in the car, she saw the dark breath of the future – corpses in the street, Berlin burning, rubble everywhere. Then she passed out. They would take her to the hospital only when they were sure she was already dead.

The Rigorous Sadness of Erik Satie

He didn't permit visitors to his one-room apartment in the 27 years he lived there. After his death (from drink), the landlord let in friends and family. They discovered a room littered with more than 100 umbrellas. There were two grand pianos, one placed on top of the other. He had used the upper piano as storage, not only for letters, parcels, and old newspapers, but also for the kind of noises an audience would pay not to hear — sirens, taxi horns, a jack in the box. Behind the piano, they found a gray velvet suit he thought he had forgotten on a bus years ago. In the pockets were notes to himself. On one was written, "Shake like a leaf"; on another, "Be invisible for a moment."

Oscar Wilde's Teeth

The tooth has to come out. Every surgeon he consulted said so. An infection had dissolved the bone around tooth number 13. He would get an electric shock of sorts when he ate or drank. Even talking could trigger a jolt of pain. And yet he couldn't resist the urge to wiggle the tooth with his tongue. After surgery, he was left with an embarrassing gap where the tooth had been and would often speak with his hand in front of his mouth. Only very rarely would he smile. He was like a book of jokes and riddles whose pages were stuck together.

Art for Art's Sake

When Henri Matisse was an old man,
too feeble to handle a paintbrush any
longer or even get himself out of bed,
he rubbed some charcoal on the end
of a pointer stick and drew on the ceiling –
it had just seemed so chillingly empty.

French Cool

Given the choice, I would want to be the sort of shrewd, goatish old man Rodin was and, after a productive morning in the studio, stroll the broad boulevards and ornate arcades of Paris with a young Russian-born French lady leaning lightly on my arm, and if her eyes were too wide apart for her to be considered a classic beauty, or if she hadn't actually read any of the books I had recommended, I wouldn't mind, because fall weather would have arrived, and the air would be like crisp white wine, and we would always feel at least a little drunk.

Advice for the Perplexed

Wash your sex toys (your unmotorized ones, at any rate) in the top of the dishwasher. Have a trick for getting bong water out of the carpet; white wine, ironically, gets out red wine stains. Try to avoid being carried off by a UFO when you can just walk. However long it takes, count all the ways there are to kill a person: hanging, shooting, stabbing, drowning, poisoning, beheading, stoning. . . Make mute despair your default greeting to people you pass on the stairs. And always remember, a wild bull becomes docile if tethered to a fig tree.

The End of Nature

I fell asleep to the rat-tat-tat of rain and dreamed I could breathe underwater. The grieving came later, when they cut open the belly of a stranded whale and found coins and plastic water bottles inside. Then I learned there could be such a thing as too much sun. Now I'm wondering what comes next, if we'll only be able to view nature in assigned locations. You'll go and sit in a darkened theater, surrounded by dozens of strangers, and when you start to sob, not even half the people there will understand.

The Third Reich of Dreams

I dreamed that it was forbidden to dream, but that I did anyway. In the morning the phone rang. A dull voice said, "This is the Monitoring Office." I started begging and pleading that this one time I be forgiven – please just don't report anything this one time, don't pass it on, please just forget it. The voice remained absolutely silent and then hung up. Over the next few days, street signs were replaced on every corner with posters proclaiming, in white letters on a black background, the 20 words peoples weren't allowed to say. The first was "Lord"; the last was "I."

Heartsick

The doctor is absurdly talkative. "Apparently it's Mental Health Awareness Day today," he says. "And ski season is coming. I've never been to California and, yes, that's sad." He keeps up his chattering while jamming a giant needle into my chest. I beg him, "Stop, stop, please stop." He just pushes the needle in deeper. I'm screaming now. A nurse hurries in. "Almost there," the doctor calmly tells her, referring, I imagine in my distress, to the outskirts of hell, where fallen angels, some the size of grains of salt, some the size of a pebbles, buzz like dung flies.

Well, Well, Well

God arrived on the 5:15 train. I met him at the station. His hollow-cheeked face faintly resembled Julius Caesar's. As I drove him downtown he stared morosely out the window at the approaching skyline. "That abominable steeple," he muttered as a popular church came into view. I had always assumed that he enjoyed indulging in the violence of a fascist thug, but he didn't seem particularly belligerent or vicious, just tired and sad. He acted, if anything, like he didn't believe he ought to exist.

Myths of the Near Future

The last surviving shul is being converted to use as a tool shed. Out front a noose has been looped around the neck of a statue of Anne Frank. We're approaching the hour when torturers report in for the night shift. Meanwhile, some 2,000 women and girls rally in the park against menstruation. Young soldiers accompanied by snarling German shepherds patrol the crowd, the soldiers forbidden on pain of death to make friends with the dogs.

Claw

There's a lump about the size of a marble under the skin of my left palm. I showed it to my brother, a doctor, when he dropped by the house. He felt the lump, pressed it, asked me if it hurt. He said I had something called Dupuytren's Contracture. As I age, my fingers will contract inwards. Eventually my hand will turn into a kind of useless claw. I won't be able to put my hand in my pocket anymore or pick up a coffee cup with it or cup her breast. I'll have to learn to grasp at straws with just one hand.

The View from Here

I'm dusting the indoor plants when the doorbell rings. It's you, and you're bleeding from an ear. "What happened to your ear?" I ask. You touch it. Your fingers come away with blood. "Steely Dan on the headphones," you say with a shrug. I don't move, don't even nod. Now that an estimated 150 species go extinct every day, I try not to rush through my days. And if, as sometimes happens, it feels like everything is speeding up, I'll lie down on the floor and stare at the ceiling or out the window, my view a small thing but my own.

Fire Burns Upwards

We see and smell the smoke all day. I'm scared to breathe in. People are crying, shoving, tripping, trying to leave, scrambling everywhere. Within a year or less, strangers will move into our houses. They'll try on our clothes, put on our jewelry. They'll replace the photographs on the walls and tabletops with their own. Hundreds can be doing this at one time. Thousands! The only evidence that we might have once existed will be the shoe that someone lost while fleeing.

Safety Instructions for the Twenty-First Century

It probably won't look like the real you. Stay calm when you come upon it. Face it and stand upright. Speak firmly to it. Do what you can to appear larger – raise your arms or open your jacket if you're wearing one. You want to convince it you are not prey and may, in fact, be a danger to it. Give it a way to escape, but if it attacks, don't panic and run. People have fought it with rocks, sticks, caps or jackets, garden tools, and their bare hands. So remain standing or at least try to get back up.

A New Kind of Heaven

The hangman was drunk on the job. A sheriff's deputy had to climb up to press the button that triggered the trap door. It was 1936 and the last public execution in the United States. A medical student conducted the autopsy. He took out the intestines, said, "Yep, it's all there," and then shoved them back in. The body was buried in a secret location for reasons that have never been satisfactorily explained. Today we go about these things entirely differently. An osprey passes overhead with steady, languid wingbeats while clutching in its claws a fish astonished to be flying.

A Hazy Shade of Postcolonial Melancholia

Is it still winter where you are? Do you have a dancing monkey to help you get through it? I was born semi-depressed in the middle of the 20th century. Veiled figures have accompanied my entire life. It's been hard work for them, but, as Charlie Chan says, "Nut easy to crack often empty." Everything will make some kind of sense when a Soviet era spacecraft, six decades after launch, finally splashes down in a neighbor's aboveground pool with the dog astronaut aboard. Until then, an elephant is dreaming of its childhood in the bush, far away from the circus.

Kiss Your Ass Goodbye

There are always more volunteers than available spots on the firing squad. But the really terrible part isn't how cold it is out. It's how much I tremble. The I Ching advises, "Wait in the meadow," meaning caring for a cow will bring luck. I can remember a time when everyone wasn't in such a hurry to fuck off to somewhere. Now, whatever phone number I punch in, the suicide hotline picks up. I think about mentioning this to someone. And then I get distracted by the wind and the rain and the loud kissing noises they seem to make.

Grandson

Now that you're 8, you have to know how to travel on foot. You have to know how to make fire without matches. You have to know how to catch a trout with your bare hands. (It's fairly easy. You just have to understand how the trout thinks.) You have to know how to forge a document, let's say a gun permit, in a country under military rule. You have to know how to open a safety lock — surreptitiously. of course, with burglar tools. More important, you have to know how to tell at a glance night from other darkness.

The Importance of Listening

I went on my own because I couldn't get anyone to come with me. What had once been an orchard was now a graveyard for old tires, sprung mattresses, rusty paint cans, even broken microwaves, scattered over the slope like the indecipherable wreckage of some puzzling event. The trees, untended for years, had long since stopped producing apples and been twisted into painful shapes and then overwhelmed by creeper vines and the depredations of opportunistic birds and insects. I just stood with my head cocked to one side as if trying to catch every single word the crows said.

Wheatfield with Crows

He presented himself at Licensed Brothel No. 1 and asked with formal politeness for the girl named Rachel. When she appeared, dressed for work in stockings and a slip, he handed her his ear (or, more precisely, the lower half of his left ear, wrapped in cloth). "Guard this object carefully," he said, and you would've thought he was bestowing on her a masterpiece of art. Then he turned and walked away. She was accustomed to freaky requests from clients, but this was a first. The police said call if it happened again.

Oh, Mercy

I board the subway at 72nd Street carrying a briefcase like the one that contains secret nuclear launch codes. A busker playing guitar at the far end of the car is trying to make up in enthusiasm what he lacks in talent. He apparently adheres to Lou Reed's dictum: anything with more than three chords is jazz. The passengers ignore his musical pleas for attention. They nap. They text. They shed virus. When the train emerges for a moment above ground, the sky looks as if it's been digitally erased. There are colors in nature that birds can see, but humans can't.

The Ladder

There are days when I look up from some small task – answering a text or fixing a cup of coffee or leashing the dog – and see miles more of the skyline burning and crowds chanting encouragement to the flames. On those days, I feel broken and hollow and lost – too old and slow to be able to make any sort of difference. Then I remember I don't have to be one of the ones who climb the rescue ladder; I can stand on the ground and help hold the ladder steady.

Love Note

Even though the sign says, "Do Not Swim Near Seals," we'll have fun, go on a picnic in the hills, maybe spend the whole night there, so many stars that the sky looks perforated by cosmic buckshot; or we'll sleep in and then helicopter over traffic jams, moving, breathing, shining from rehab center to wedding cake palace, while the angel of death rolls a cigarette and the border wall sinks another quarter of an inch; and this will happen again and again, people turning up at all hours to complain bitterly about being written out of our story.

The Carnival of Being

It's so bleak outside that I decide to hide for the day in my little room. The other first-floor tenant has removed his clothes and walked off down the street. I can't stop replaying in my head the saddest sound in the world: a shovelful of soil thumping the lid of a coffin. For now, at least, there's no great difference between a funeral and a carnival. Volunteer firefighters have been going around the neighborhood distributing oxygen masks for pets. Asthma sufferers, especially. That's the problem with people who put Velveeta on enchiladas – they can't tell anymore what's appropriate. By evening, white hairs have sprouted on just one side of my mustache.

Pastiche

The scene is a synagogue, but has nothing to do with religion. When you look at this at a distance, you can't tell whether it's upside down or right side up — you can't tell what's here. The color leaves the eye. The voice becomes ugly. And the body. The hair. The fingernails. The shoes. Now get closer, put on your reading glasses. Someone suggests it's a typo. That's how the Nazis viewed their victims.

Hotel of Forgotten Artists

There's no one at the reception desk to welcome you. There never is. Only you don't realize that. How could you? And so you wait. You wait and wait, and while you wait, your clothes, your manner, your worldview go out of fashion. Only you don't realize that either. By now you don't even realize that you are waiting, because you have been waiting so long that waiting has become indistinguishable from being. Nothing ever disrupts or otherwise interferes with the industry of waiting. No one crosses the lobby. No one sits on the furniture placed in conversation clusters. No news enters from outdoors. It's been a year, maybe more, since you last imagined you heard voices, footsteps, music. Upstairs the rooms are spotless – in fact, identical white boxes – and all numbered zero.

The three poems that follow are based on tape recordings of a series of classes photographer Diane Arbus gave in 1971.

Devolving

I could become
a million things:

child with a toy
hand grenade
in Central Park,

identical twins,

a flower girl
at a wedding,

nudist lady
with swan
sun glasses,

Xmas tree
in a living room.

I don't like
to arrange things.

If I stand in front
of something,

instead of arranging it
I arrange myself.

Certain Machines

I don't feel that total identity with the machine.
I mean I can work it fine,
although I'm not so great actually.

Sometimes when I'm winding it,
it'll get stuck or something will go wrong
and I just start clicking everything
and suddenly very often it's alright again.

That's my feeling about machines.
You sort of look the other way,
they'll get fixed. Except for certain ones.

The Flaw

1
There was a dog that came
at twilight every day.
A big dog. Kind of a mutt.
He would come and just stare at me.
I mean a dog, not barking, not licking,
just looking right through you.
I don't particularly like dogs.
Well, I love stray dogs,
dogs who don't like people.
And that's the kind of dog picture
I would take if I ever took a dog picture.

2
Nothing
is ever the same
as they said
it was.
It's what I've
never seen before
that I recognize.
It's a little bit
like walking
into a hallucination
without being
quite sure
whose it is.

3
You see someone on the street
and what you notice about them is the flaw.
It's just extraordinary that we should

have been given these peculiarities.
And, not content with what we're given,
we create a whole other set.

And that's what all this is a little about.
That somebody else's tragedy
is not the same as your own.

Orogeny

Everyone assumes that paper always defeats rock. Do the math! This life is dangerous. I was taught to never begin a sentence with "and" or "but" when I really should have been taught to never begin a sentence. Or maybe I just misheard the instructions while the volcanoes in my head erupted. How would you describe me to a stranger? Maligned? Bereft? A hovel made from sheets of plywood and tin? What a story it all makes – if you change the details around. Even a dictatorship ends eventually, but a story is sort of like a self-replicating virus, a bee with pollen caught in its fur, a voice that flees to the woods and lives as a bandit.

The Heart of It All

Her eyes were sometimes blue, sometimes green with flecks of gold, all the things, restless things, I was instructed from early on never to do. We found a window filled with scenes night and day and lay down under it and moved slowly, so slowly that by morning we had rubbed each other as smooth as sea-smoothed shells. And when we rose up, the world looked strange. It was a place of beauty, I can tell you that, a circular path, spiraling even, and no one was really sure why but us.

In Excelsis Gloria

My daughter 13 comes home
from school her dark eyes darker
than usual as if the irises had crystallized
because the chorus has been practicing
singing that song In Excelsis Gloria
for the winter concert she says no way
can she it weirds her out to call Jesus
Lord Savior the chorus teacher
when she told him shook his head
deal with it he said and there it is
like the dead bird Xylophone our cat
leaves by the front door as a gift
oddly without a mark of violence on it
or any blood just small enough
to fit into my pocket and carry away
if I wish a soft weight a terrible reminder
a secret love note scribbled in haste

Lovesick

It isn't love if our embassy isn't burning,
if the windows haven't exploded

in a shower of diamonds from the heat,
if the ballerina isn't staggering around onstage

as from an accidental elbow in the face,
or if the knife thrower, subject to ironic applause,

doesn't suddenly doubt the accuracy of his aim;
it isn't love if the moon isn't breathing,

if we don't receive unsought help from machines,
an automated summons to appear in court

and our bewildered joy upon entering the night
a moment after everyone else has left.

Acknowledgments

The author wishes to thank the editors of the following journals and presses in which many of the poems in this collection originally appeared, often in different form:

Revolution John
ubu
Beatnik Cowboy
Otoliths
New World Writing
Apocalypse Confidential
A Story in 100 Words
Ice Floe
One Art
433
Spinozablue
Bombfire
Right Hand Pointing
Unbroken
One Sentence Poems
Press Americana
Grey Book Press
Alien Buddha Press
Laughing Ronin Press
King Fu Treachery Press

About the Author

Howie Good, professor emeritus of Digital Media and Journalism at SUNY New Paltz, is the author of some dozen poetry collections, including most recently *The Horses Were Beautiful* (2022) from Grey Book Press. He is the winner of the Lorien Poetry Prize from Thoughtcrime Press for *The Loser's Guide to Street Fighting* and the Press Americana Prize for Poetry for *Dangerous Acts Starring Unstable Elements*. He co-edits the journal Unbroken, dedicated to prose poetry.

www.ingramcontent.com/pod-product-compliance
Lightning Source LLC
Chambersburg PA
CBHW020945090426
42736CB00010B/1268